THE BA
LEXINGTON AND CONCORD

A History from Beginning to End

Table of Contents

Introduction

July 4, 1776 is the date most immediately associated with the American War of Independence against the British, but a date that's equally important in the saga is April 19, 1775. It was on that day that the Sons of Liberty, having learned that the British were on their way to the towns of Lexington and Concord to capture the weapons that were stored there, set in motion the events that would erupt into the war for liberty.

It was typical of this war that the men and women who were the initial fuse for the explosion of the war were everyday sorts, not military heroes. A silversmith and a tanner set forth to alert the people of Concord and Lexington that, as Henry Wadsworth Longfellow's poem read, the British were coming. But there was nothing poetic about the course of events that would set the young colonies and their untried military forces against the spit-and-polish discipline of the British Empire's forces.

A British military force of 700 men marched to Lexington then Concord to find the hidden stores of weapons and ammunition that, unknown to Great Britain's General Gage, had already been moved to a safer place by the local citizens. No one gave the order to fire at Lexington, but someone did fire, and eight colonials were killed. It was a different matter at Concord, however, as more and more militia and minutemen continued to arrive from neighboring towns and then from neighboring states to add to the numbers of citizen soldiers waiting for the unsuspecting British to head back to Boston.

As the British column marched away, they were harried and shot at by the colonial forces whose fighting style—darting behind rocks and hills, firing and then advancing to meet the professional soldiers at the next bend in the road—lacked the precision and formation of European military fashion but was nevertheless brutally effective on the hilly, sloping terrain of New England. Even a rescue by Hugh Percy and his men did not bring the British the victory they expected, and they returned to Boston a worn-out force.

By the next morning, the city was encircled by 15,000 militiamen, and General Gage—despite his best intentions and all his efforts to maintain a decorous civility with the Bostonians—found himself in what had become, overnight, a war zone. The American Revolution had begun.

Chapter One

Taxes and Tyranny

"When liberty is the prize who would shun the warfare? Who would stoop to waste a coward thought on life?"

—Joseph Warren

Until the Battles of Lexington and Concord on April 19, 1775, the steadily escalating hostilities between the British forces in Massachusetts and their colonial brethren had mostly been a series of spontaneous responses to unpopular legislative acts passed by Parliament in London, far away from the North American continent. London failed to realize that colonial resentment against British taxes ran deep in the citizens of Boston, whose port was their livelihood. The bustling Boston Harbor was filled with ships whose cargo brought prosperity to the city and wealth to merchants like John Hancock. Hancock was a leader in Boston, the wealthiest citizen in the colony of Massachusetts, and a member of the Sons of Liberty, a Patriot organization dedicated to American independence.

From the British perspective, Massachusetts was merely a colony of the British Empire and, as such, subject to the will—and the whims—of King George III and the British Parliament. To the British, the cost of protecting the colonies during the recent war against the French and their Native American allies was something that the colonials ought to absorb. The taxes imposed upon the colonials were not excessive, they thought, and besides, British coffers needed to be replenished after the seven years of fighting.

The French and Indian War, also known as the Seven Years' War, ended in 1763. It was at that point that the British, determined to prove that they were the master, and the colonies, convinced that they were being treated unfairly, came into disagreement. The next year, after the Treaty of Paris and the Proclamation of 1763 were signed, the new boundaries of the continent were set. The land west of the Appalachian Mountains was denied to restless American settlers notable for their wanderlust and was designated for the native tribes who were already dwelling there. Those new territories would have administrative costs, and remaining debts from the years of fighting needed to be paid.

Parliament passed the Grenville Acts with the goal of raising the money and initiating measures designed to make the customs system more efficient. The Sugar Act, passed in 1764, increased duties on a variety of items that were in common use in the colony, including textiles, coffee, and sugar. The colonials were incensed and met to discuss the injustice of having taxes levied against them when they had no representation in Parliament. Convinced that in order to combat the tax they needed to make the British feel the pinch in their pocketbooks, the merchants of Boston initiated a nonimportation policy, boycotting British luxury goods, a tactic which spread to other colonies as well.

The British were unimpressed, and 1765 saw the implementation of the first direct tax imposed upon the colonials. The Stamp Act was even more unpopular than the Sugar Act. The passing of the Quartering Act, which forced colonial citizens to provide quarters for the British troops stationed there, further added to the friction. Virginia's House of Burgesses and its fiery orator Patrick Henry held that only Virginia could tax Virginians. Through Committees of Correspondence, the colonial citizens were proactive in spreading the word of how the British were inflicting what seemed like tyrannical acts against the people of the Thirteen Colonies.

Through the summer, organizations formed to resist the stamp agents charged with enforcing the tax. Known as the Sons of Liberty, the members of these organizations did not hesitate to use violence in order to achieve their ends. In the fall, New York City hosted the Stamp Act Congress with representation from nine of the thirteen colonies. The representatives wrote a petition to deliver to King George III to express their objections.

When the Stamp Act went into effect on November 1, the colonists were resolved not to use the stamps, bringing business hurtling to a halt. The tactic was ultimately successful as the British repealed the Stamp Act on March 18, 1766. But, loathe to relinquish power, the government passed the Declaratory Act, a measure which authorized the British to legislate any colonial laws.

When the New York Assembly refused to provide the funds needed to quarter British troops, the British suspended the legislature. For the colonial citizens who had grown accustomed to governing themselves, the suspension was an ominous reminder that regardless of what freedoms they enjoyed, they remained subject to a powerful overlord which had control over their fate.

The tug of war between British presumption of authority and colonial concepts of independence continued into 1767. Mid-year saw Parliament pass the Townsend Acts, which imposed duties on tea, glass, and paper. Parliament also established the means by which these external taxes could be enforced. Boston, in retaliation, reinstated the nonimportation of British goods.

The British were less than pleased in 1768 when Samuel Adams, one of the most influential of the Sons of Liberty and a former tax collector himself, wrote a letter opposing the Townsend Acts. The letter was sent with the approval of the Massachusetts Assembly and traveled to other colonies, where it won support from other colonial legislatures.

When John Hancock's ship *Liberty* was seized in 1768 as a result of a dispute over customs violations, Bostonians responded with threats of violence against the customs officials, who then sent a request for more British troops. Late in September, the British warships arrived, and two regiments entered the city to enforce the hated laws.

Although the other colonies were not necessarily in sync with the radicals of Boston, they were concerned that British authority might at some point interfere with their own self-government. On May 7, 1769, nonimportation resolutions were submitted to the Virginia House of Burgesses by one of the colony's leading citizens, George Washington. When the British dissolved the Virginia House of Burgesses after other Virginians sent proclamations to the British king, the delegates, unbowed, gathered at the Raleigh Tavern in Williamsburg to endorse the nonimportation agreement.

Then, a snowy night in March 1770 led to bloodshed when a Boston mob harassed and provoked members of the British military who were guarding the Customs House. Shooting began, although the leader of the unit, Captain Thomas Preston, had told his men not to fire. The death of five Bostonians, with six others injured, would lead to a trial in which six of the soldiers were acquitted of the charge of murder; two others were branded on the thumb, escaping the death sentence. Leading their defense in court was John Adams, cousin to the more volatile Samuel. Samuel Adams was not pleased with the final verdict, but he managed to turn the episode into a propaganda win that has endured to this day, as the event is still known as the Boston Massacre.

It seemed that circumstances had reached a dangerous point, and the British did not wish to exacerbate matters—nor did they wish to surrender their authority. Their compromise was to repeal the Townsend Acts, except for the tax on tea.

By November of 1772, Samuel Adams was orchestrating a Committee of Correspondence that would be in contact with other towns in Massachusetts to keep the communities apprised of British threats to the self-governing practice of the colony. Samuel Adams was proving himself to be a master of intelligence, keeping the local areas current on the ever-simmering tensions between the British and the Bostonians. So effective was the Committee of Correspondence that by 1774, eleven of the thirteen colonies had their own; only North Carolina and Pennsylvania did not.

The Tea Act, which went into effect in May 1773, was established so that the East India Company could recoup some of its financial losses by underselling colonial merchants. The Bostonians were irate at the issuing of an import tax on tea, and the year ended with the Boston Tea Party, where Bostonians dressed as Mohawk Indians boarded ships in Boston Harbor to dump tea into the ocean.

Retribution was inevitable; the "Mohawks" had dumped what would be, in today's money, the equivalent of $1.4 million worth of tea into the harbor, and Great Britain was not going to let this pass without response. The Coercive Acts of 1774 included a bill which closed Boston Harbor to trade; the only goods that could go through the port until the cost of the tea was paid for by the city were military supplies and other cargo that the British approved.

More punishment followed. General Gage, the commander of all British forces in the colonies, entered Boston with four regiments. A new Quartering Act was passed while General Gage seized the arsenal of the Massachusetts Colony.

Massachusetts was declared to be in a state of rebellion in February, but later that same month, Parliament backtracked on its punitive actions and removed a number of the taxes which so vexed the colonies. By this time, however, taxes were no longer the sole irritant causing friction between the mother country and her unruly colonies. In Virginia, Patrick Henry was already proclaiming, "Give me liberty or give me death."

Chapter Two

The Rebellion in Massachusetts

"A part of your Majesty's subjects, in the Province of the Massachusetts Bay, have proceeded so far to resist the authority of the supreme Legislature."

—British Parliament

For the British government, the obstinance of the Massachusetts colony was insulting and threatening, and in an address to King George III in February 1775, both Houses of Parliament expressed their concerns. The colony was resisting authority, and while Parliament was willing, it said, to listen to any real grievances which were brought to its attention, the laws of Great Britain had to be obeyed. If the colony of Massachusetts Bay chose not to obey those laws, then obedience would need to be enforced.

Parliament instructed General Thomas Gage, who was also serving as the governor of the colony, to disarm the rebels and put the leaders in prison. Parliament did allow General Gage some leverage in his decisions, perhaps aware that the British officer was dealing with a delicate and difficult set of circumstances.

In 1758, Gage had married Margaret Kemble, the well-connected daughter of a New Jersey businessman and his wife, who was the granddaughter of a judge. The Kembles were affluent and influential, and their daughter was loyal to her colony as well as to the country of her husband's birth and had said that she "hoped her husband would never be the instrument of sacrificing the lives of her countrymen." While the Thirteen Colonies regarded themselves as British subjects, it had seemed unlikely that there would be division with Great Britain. But new identities were being forged in the fire of what Parliament regarded as rebellion.

Gage was doing his utmost to maintain order and peace in the tumultuous colony. He had learned from a spy in the Provincial Congress that Massachusetts had sent messages to the other New England colonies, seeking help to raise 18,000 fighting men.

The colonies had long been on their own when it came to defending themselves. The nature of living in North America required New England citizens, as well as those of other colonies, to rely on themselves when it came to protecting their people and property. From the very beginning of settlement in the New World, colonial militias had been formed to provide defense against attacks by Native tribes. A scant 16 years after the first English settlers landed in what would become Massachusetts Colony, an alliance of New England settlements and Native American allies was at war with the Pequot tribe. The governor at that time called for the raising of a militia to meet the threat in 1636.

Again in 1660, settlements from Maine to New York's frontier were threatened by the Narragansett, Pequot, Wampanoag, Pennacook, and Abenaki tribes. The Native

Americans, faced with the invasion of their lands as well as disease and hunger, met the threat of the newcomers invading their hunting grounds. The colonial forces were not a polished unit, and their weapons, the pike and the matchlock, were primitive. Still, by 1675, the settlements had established local militias to meet the danger and had built forts along the coast.

The settlers knew that they faced a dire threat. Chief Metacomet (also known as King Philip) had become the leader of the Wampanoag Confederacy in 1662, and in order to defend his people, he forged tribal alliances with the intention of forcing the Europeans from the continent. On June 24, 1675, the Native Americans attacked a town in Plymouth, and King Philip's War was underway. Although the settlers were ultimately victorious and the Native Americans suffered massacres and a diminution of their numbers, the Native Americans still wreaked destruction on the colonists, attacking more than half of the 90 settlements in the region, destroying a dozen of them.

While the threat of tribal attacks had eased in the late eighteenth century in New England, the colonial militias that had formed were by no means incompetent, even if they were rustic and unpolished in comparison to the British forces. Colonial forces had also fought alongside British troops during the battles of the French and Indian War, which had just ended in 1763. Each New England colony required all of its towns to form militias comprised of all males over the age of 16 up to age 60 and to provide weapons for the soldiers.

The provincial government of Massachusetts was the authority under which the militias served, although the companies throughout New England were responsible for electing their officers themselves. Leadership and authority were handled very differently in the colonies than they were in Great Britain, and this fissure would prove to be a key point of friction as the two sides became ever more entrenched in opposite philosophies of governance.

In order to remain battle-ready, the militias would assemble as an entire unit in each town from two to four times a year during peacetime for training. They would expand that schedule to three to four times a week when the threat of war was growing nearer.

In October 1774, the Massachusetts Provincial Congress took note of the British buildup of military force. It counted 17,000 men in the colony's militia, fewer than they regarded as necessary for their defense. They applied to other New England governments to add to their numbers and increase the efficacy of the militia. The Congress suggested that the militias designate one-quarter of their force as soldiers who were to be equipped and ready to march to battle with minimal notice. Known as minutemen, they were to be divided into companies of at least 50 men each.

In 1774, militia companies were called out to protect the stores of ammunition, but by the time the militia was ready to go, British troops had already captured weapons at Cambridge and Charlestown and were back in Boston.

The Massachusetts militias had been gathering weapons and other supplies at Concord and Worcester, and they knew that it was likely that the British would be marching from Boston to capture the ammunition there as well. As far away as Philadelphia, colonists were aware that the

British were intent on capturing the militia's armaments. The *Pennsylvania Journal* reported that the British were supposed to be going to Concord because "a quantity of provision and warlike stores are lodged there."

Although the British controlled Boston, Massachusetts' leaders had adopted the Suffolk Resolves after the Boston Tea Party and formed the Massachusetts Provincial Congress. Outside of Boston, which was under British rule, the Massachusetts Provincial Congress had, in effect, control of the colony. This led the British government to declare that Massachusetts was in a state of rebellion.

On March 30, 1775, the Massachusetts Provincial Congress declared that when the British troops under General Gage's command marched from Boston, the Province's military force was to assemble and act defensively.

By April 8, 1775, the radical leaders of Boston had left the city, recognizing the danger that they faced by the British if they stayed. General Gage was particularly eager to capture Samuel Adams and John Hancock, who had escaped from Boston to stay with a Hancock relative to avoid the threat of arrest.

But not all of the Sons of Liberty were gone. Paul Revere and Joseph Warren remained in Boston, and they had learned, through their own network of spies, that General Gage had received instructions from London. In fact, they received the news before Gage did. Privy to the news, the Sons of Liberty had removed most of the supplies from Concord to other locations, although that was the site where the British expected to find armaments. What the British did not expect to find was an ever-increasing number of colonial militiamen prepared to defend their ground against a hostile military force.

Chapter Three

The British Are Coming!

"One if by land, and two if by sea;
And I on the opposite shore will be,
Ready to ride and spread the alarm."

—Henry Wadsworth Longfellow, "Paul Revere's Ride"

What was intended to be a secret mission by the British to capture and destroy the weapons and ammunition that were believed to be concealed in Concord had already been revealed to Boston patriots weeks before General Gage received the orders from London. Poised for action, the Sons of Liberty waited for the signal that would send them into action and, although they did not know it, would lead the colonies to war.

On the morning of April 18, 1775, General Gage ordered a mounted patrol to go out into the countryside to catch any messengers from Boston who might be delivering news of the British plans to march on Concord. Sending British soldiers out into the outlying areas of Boston was nothing new; General Gage had done it before in an effort to find out where John Hancock and Samuel Adams, the rabble-rousers of the rebellion, were staying. But this time, the patrol behaved differently and the residents were alarmed, heightening their apprehension as well as their awareness, as by this time everyone knew that trouble was on the horizon.

That afternoon, Lieutenant-Colonel Francis Smith, in command of 700 British Army regulars, received orders from General Gage; however, he was told that he was not to read the instructions until his troops were in motion. Gage was operating with a heightened sense of security, fearing that if the movements of the troops were detected, the militias would converge by the thousands, putting the British forces in danger. Gage had 6,000 troops under his command, but if militias from all over New England learned of the British plans, he nevertheless risked being outnumbered.

Gage was ever sensitive to the fact that the colonists were British subjects, and he reminded Smith of this fact. The British troops were not permitted to effect any destruction of property nor to plunder the citizenry. Gage, knowing the temper of the colony, did not even issue written orders to arrest the leaders of the nascent rebellion, recognizing that if they were arrested, an uprising might result.

Although the ringleaders of the Boston rebellion had left the city, fearing for their lives and safety if they were captured, there were still representatives remaining in Boston, including the physician Joseph Warren, who numbered Mrs. Gage among his friends, silversmith Paul Revere, and tanner William Dawes. Warren had a well-placed source within the British command from whom he learned that this was the night, April 18, when the British would march on Concord.

General Gage met with his senior officers at the Province House at dusk to update them on the orders he'd received to move against the colonial rebels. Lieutenant-Colonel Smith would command the force with Major John Pitcairn serving as his executive officer.

After the meeting adjourned at 8:30 pm, one of the officers, Brigadier-General Hugh Percy, also known as Earl Percy, was out on the Boston Common, where he overheard the other townspeople discussing the movement of the British troops. One of the citizens said that the British would not succeed in their goal of obtaining the cannon at Concord. Percy quickly informed Gage of what he had learned. Gage immediately sent orders to keep any local messengers from getting out of the city, but he was too late.

On the night of April 18, 1775, between nine and ten o'clock, Joseph Warren was in contact with Paul Revere and William Dawes, alerting them that the British were heading out of Boston for Cambridge, where they would take the road to Lexington and Concord. Warren's source believed that the reason for the march was to hunt for Adams and Hancock. The Sons of Liberty weren't concerned about the weapons in Concord, which had been removed to safety earlier, but Warren knew that the militias of Lexington and the surrounding areas were probably unaware that the British were on the hunt. He wanted Dawes and Revere to warn them.

Historians are uncertain of the identity of the source who provided Warren with the information about the British plans, but there is some speculation that the person might have been Margaret Kemble Gage, the general's wife. Gage himself said that only two people knew of the plans, one of which was his second in command. Was the other person his wife? The Gages were a close couple and parents to eleven children, but after the military action against Lexington and Concord went awry, Gage sent his wife back to Britain.

Warren sent Revere and Dawes to deliver the message to Concord that British troops were on their way. The two couriers would travel by separate routes in case either man was captured. Revere would travel across the Charles River by boat to get to Charlestown, where patriots would be waiting for a signal regarding the route the British would take.

The patriots knew that the British would be leaving Boston for Concord, but what they didn't know was whether the troops would travel by land or sea. They would learn the route of the British by watching for a signal from the steeple of the Old North Church, which was the highest point in the city of Boston. One lantern in the steeple would indicate that the British were coming by land; two lanterns meant that the troops were traveling by sea.

Revere had instructed three men to hang the lanterns in the steeple. Church sexton Robert Newman and Captain John Pulling each carried a lantern while Thomas Bernard stood guard outside the church watching in case British troops came by. Across the Charles River, patriots in Charlestown were waiting to see what the lanterns would reveal about the means of transportation that the British would use to get to Concord.

The lanterns would only hang for less than a minute to avoid detection by the British. The militiamen knew what to look for and were ready to go as soon as they spotted the twin lights in the steeple. The British would travel by boat across the Charles River and land near the Phipps Farm.

The couriers split up; Revere, after giving his instructions to the church sextons regarding the lanterns, went north, crossing the Charles River by rowboat, unseen by the British warship HMS *Somerset.* Bostonians were forbidden to cross the river at that hour of the night, but Revere landed safely in Charlestown, then headed west to Lexington, informing the residents in most of the houses along the route that the British were on their way. In addition, Charlestown patriots also sent out riders with the message.

Dawes, going south, went across Boston Neck and over the Great Bridge by horse to Lexington.

It was a night of watchfulness on the part of the citizens. Dr. Samuel Prescott was in Lexington that night, visiting his fiancée. He had another purpose as well: to report on the status of Concord, its readiness for battle, the status of the hidden munitions, and its success in moving its cannon to Groton to keep it away from the British.

In addition to warning the citizens of the towns surrounding Boston that the British were coming, the couriers had another important mission: to alert Hancock and Adams of the danger they were in so that they could be moved to what is now Burlington. Later, they would be moved to Billerica. Upon arrival in Lexington, Revere and Dawes met with Hancock and Adams to discuss the situation. They were sure that the British intended to do more than just search for the latter two leaders—a force that large surely had Concord in its sights.

Prescott was leaving Lexington at around one o'clock in the morning on April 19 when he met Revere and Dawes. The two men had just left Lexington and were en route to Concord to alert the citizens that the British were marching. As the three men headed to Hartwell's Tavern, they were intercepted by four members of the British troops, part of a larger scouting party that had left the evening before.

Although Revere was captured, Prescott and Dawes escaped. However, Dawes was thrown from his horse and only Prescott was able to make it to Concord. Prescott went to the tavern and told the tavernkeeper that the British were coming. Hartwell sent a slave to inform his parents who lived down the road. Mrs. Hartwell got the message to Captain William Smith, who commanded the local minutemen. The warning gave the minutemen the time they needed to reach the Old North Bridge in Concord before the British realized that the colonial forces had surprises of their own in store.

Chapter Four

The Battle of Lexington

"Stand your ground; don't fire unless fired upon, but if they mean to have a war, let it begin here."

—Captain John Parker

The couriers, Dawes, Revere, and Prescott, and all the others who mounted their horses to spread the news as soon as they heard it, were effective in alerting the people of the region that the British were marching. The colonial system of "alarm and muster" was an effective emergency response system. Not only were riders delivering the messages, but from town to town, bells, drums, alarm guns, bonfires, and even a trumpet were put to use. So effective was the operation that the British Army was still unloading its vessels in Cambridge while towns as far as 25 miles from Boston knew that the British were on the march. It was a night in motion as militias prepared for what would become the start of the American War of Independence.

The British plans did not include an altercation in Lexington. They intended to march through the town on their way to Concord, where they expected to find hidden weapons stashed by the colonial rebels. They didn't know that colonial couriers had been diligent in spreading the news that they were in the area.

The men of the Lexington militia had stayed awake through most of the night based on the warning that they had received from Paul Revere's message, but as the minutes and hours ticked by, the colonial leaders started to wonder if they had received accurate information. It was not until 4:15 am that one of the scouts sent out by Lexington militia leader Captain John Parker came back to let the militia know that the British were coming in force and that they were not far away.

Realizing that he could not win this encounter with his few men, and secure in the knowledge that the stores in Concord had already been moved to another hiding place, Parker had to practice caution. The colony was not at war with the British yet; there had been no outbreak of hostility. He did not want to ignite a war on his own. He set his men in position, employing parade-ground formation on the Common, in plain sight, making no attempt to interfere with the British soldiers as they marched.

At sunrise on April 19, 80 members of the Lexington militia were standing in ranks on the Lexington Common as British Major John Pitcairn's advance guard entered the town. Also watching the arrival of the red-coated soldiers were between 40 to 100 spectators. Militia engagement was a family affair, and as many as one-quarter of the Lexington militia were related to their commander Parker. He was a farmer by occupation but had amassed colonial military experience, having fought in the battle for Quebec during the French and Indian War. Parker was in the final stages of tuberculosis, with only five months left to live. Not only was the disease killing him, but it had also weakened his voice, making it difficult for him to be heard, something which would prove to be a factor in the forthcoming battlefield encounter.

Both leaders—the homespun colonial soldier Parker and the British military professional Pitcairn—were well aware of the tension of the situation and were intent upon diffusing it. Parker uttered the words that would later be engraved in stone to commemorate the site. "Stand your ground; don't fire unless fired upon, but if they mean to have a war, let it begin here."

A British officer, possibly Pitcairn but it might have been another man, rode forward, sword raised, and according to accounts, shouted out to the assembled men, "Lay down your arms, you damned rebels!" Parker opted once again for the cautious approach and instructed his force to disperse. However, his voice was difficult to hear over the mounting confusion and noise, and not everyone obeyed the command.

Pitcairn had also given the order not to fire to his own men, but nonetheless, a shot rang out, its source unknown to this day. Witnesses claimed that shots were then fired from both sides, and the British began firing volleys although they had not been ordered to do so. The militiamen were unable to load their weapons to return fire and fled.

Eight colonials were killed and ten were wounded; a British soldier suffered a wound to the thigh. The British soldiers were in some disorder and, after firing their weapons, were getting ready to enter the homes of the Lexington residents. Lieutenant-Colonel Smith then arrived with the remainder of his force and was able to restore order.

The skirmish done, the British column reformed and began the march to Concord, unaware that colonial militia had mustered and were ready and waiting for them.

Chapter Five

The Battle of Concord

"Whoever looks upon them as an irregular mob will find himself much mistaken."

—Brigadier-General Hugh Percy

The militias mustered in Concord to prepare for the British, but upon receiving reports that shots were being fired at Lexington, they didn't know what to do: wait for reinforcements from the neighboring towns, remain in Concord to defend it against attack, or move east, where they could have the advantage of better terrain for their fight.

A column of the militia's men, 250 in number, marched a little more than a mile on the road to Lexington. But upon encountering 700 British regulars, the column turned around to return to Concord, 500 yards ahead of the British coming behind them. They gathered at a ridge that overlooked the town. Then the men, led by Colonel James Barrett, crossed the North Bridge a mile north of Concord, to a hill that provided a vantage point from which to watch the British in the town. As they watched, their ranks grew in size as minutemen from the towns to the west arrived.

Meanwhile, the British in Concord were following the orders from General Gage. The grenadiers of the 10th Regiment secured the South Bridge. Seven companies of light infantry, one hundred men, claimed the North Bridge, unaware that they were being watched by the militias that were gathering. Four companies were taken two miles beyond North Bridge to search for hidden weapons, as intelligence reports from spies loyal to the British had told them where to look.

Two companies were stationed as guards for their return, and one company was set to the task of guarding the bridge. All the companies were under the command of Captain Walter Laurie. The British knew that their commanding officer lacked experience, and they also knew that they were outnumbered by the militia. Recognizing the dangers of the situation, Laurie sent a request for reinforcements to Lieutenant-Colonel Smith.

Meanwhile, the soldiers who were looking for the hidden weapons ordered Ephraim Jones, the proprietor of a tavern, to show them where a cannon was reportedly buried on his property. Jones had barred his door and refused entry to the troops, but the British were not going to be put off by a barred door. Major Pitcairn ordered Jones at gunpoint to reveal the hiding place of the three large guns capable of firing 24-pound shots and sufficient range to strike Boston. The British smashed the gun trunnions so that they couldn't be mounted, then burned gun carriages they found in the Concord meetinghouse.

The burning flames led to a fire, and one of the residents convinced the British to form a bucket brigade in order to save the building. Despite the hostile nature of the attack, the British were civil to the townspeople, even while searching for the munitions. The townspeople took advantage of the courtesy and steered the troops away from some of the weapons caches that remained in the town. Although Barrett's Farm had been the storage site for weapons in the earlier weeks, most of them had been moved and buried in furrows in a field, giving the appearance of a planted crop. The mission to find weapons yielded disappointing results for the British.

When the militia troops under Colonel Barrett saw the smoke coming from the town square, they assumed that only a few light infantry companies were responsible for the flames and marched from Punkatasset Hill to a closer, lower hilltop that was 300 miles from the North Bridge. Seeing the militia advance, the two British companies holding the position near the road retreated to the bridge, yielding the hill to Barrett's militia.

More militiamen arrived from the surrounding towns, including Concord, Lincoln, Bedford, and Acton, bringing a force of 400 against the 100 or so men in Captain Laurie's light infantry companies.

Barrett instructed the men to load their weapons but not to fire them unless they were fired upon, and to advance. Laurie ordered his companies guarding the bridge to retreat; when one of the men began pulling up the bridge planks so that the colonial forces couldn't use it, Major Buttrick of the Concord militia ordered him to stop. Advancing two by two, the militia and minutemen progressed in column formation.

Laurie ordered his forces to form positions to fire behind the bridge in a column that ran perpendicular to the Concord River. Unfortunately for the British, this formation would have worked if they had been shooting into a narrow area, but not for an open path that was located behind a bridge. The British who were retreating over the bridge tried to form into a position they thought would be more suitable for the surroundings. A lieutenant in the formation's rear detected the error and sent flankers out, but only three soldiers obeyed him because he was from a different company than the men under his command while the others tried to follow Laurie's orders.

When a warning shot was fired, the other soldiers, thinking that the order had been given to fire, did so before Laurie could prevent it. Two minutemen at the head of the line on their way to the bridge were killed instantly, but the colonials continued marching. Another shot was fired by the British, then others, wounding five until Major Buttrick ordered the militia to fire. The lines, 50 yards apart, were separated by the Concord River and the bridge over it. A volley of musket fire coming from the militiamen struck the British, killing or mortally wounding three and wounding nine. The British retreated, but as they descended the near the road coming out of Bedford, they found themselves trapped, outnumbered, and outmaneuvered. They abandoned their wounded soldiers and went for safety to the grenadier companies that were returning from their search for weapons.

Colonel Barrett, as stunned as his men by their unexpected success, sent some of his men back to the hilltop and sent others, including Major Buttrick, to a defensive position on a hill behind a stone wall, across the river. When Lieutenant-Colonel Smith heard the shots not long after receiving Laurie's request for reinforcements, he led two companies of grenadiers toward the North Bridge, where they met the retreating light infantry companies.

Spotting minutemen approaching in the distance, he worried that the four companies remaining at Barrett's Farm now had no protection.

The minutemen, watching from behind the wall, had no orders to fire. One man recalled, "If we had fired, I believe we could have killed almost every officer there was in the front, but we had no orders to fire and there wasn't a gun fired."

Despite the tension of the moment, the episode had a certain comic relief as a local man, Elias Brown, who suffered from mental illness, took advantage of an entrepreneurial opportunity to sell hard cider to both the minutemen and the British.

The search of Barrett's Farm having turned up nothing much of use, the detachment of soldiers who had been sent there left and came upon the battlefield, now abandoned except for the bodies of the British who had been killed or wounded during the shooting. They crossed the bridge and returned to the town by 11:30 am, observed by the growing number of militiamen concealed in defensive positions. As the British continued to search for military supplies that had been hidden, destroying whatever they found, they didn't know that the numbers of colonial militiamen were growing. The British took time to eat lunch and left Concord in the early afternoon, but their delay in leaving had provided enough time for militiamen from the surrounding towns to reach the road that led back to Boston—the road that the British would take.

By now, there were approximately 1,000 colonial soldiers assembled. British Lieutenant-Colonel Smith sent flankers to follow a road that ended about a mile outside

Concord. The main road came to a bridge over a small stream. In order to cross the bridge, the flankers were pulled back into the main formation, closing ranks with only three soldiers abreast. The colonial forces, with their greater numbers, presented the very danger that General Gage had been so eager to avoid. The British rearguard fired a volley at the militiamen. The fire was returned and two British soldiers were killed, others wounded, with no harm inflicted upon the colonial forces.

What was especially frustrating to the British was the style of fighting that the militias employed. Instead of forming in an organized manner like the armies of Europe did, the colonials shot from behind trees and walls and whatever defensive concealment they could find. When Smith's forces charged up Hardy's Hill (also known as Brooks Hill) to drive away the militiamen who were assembled south of the road, the colonists once again fired with deadly accuracy. Smith's men withdrew from the hill, and they went forward to yet another bridge into the town of Lincoln, near Brooks Tavern. Once again, the militiamen fired upon the British.

The British reached a spot where the road rose and curved to the left through a section of woods. Here a militia company was positioned in what would become known as the "Bloody Angle" at a bend in the road in an area of rocky terrain and trees. Parallel to the road, other militias were in place; still more militia companies on the road closed it from behind. Five hundred yards further where the road curved again, more militiamen fired on the British column from opposite sides of the road. Thirty British soldiers were killed or wounded; the colonial forces only lost four.

The British then broke into a pace that was too fast for the militias to maintain in the terrain, while the forces behind the British were too densely packed together to aim at the red-coated troops. By now, the gathering militias numbered around 2,000 men. Although the road straightened and the British had more success this time in firing upon the colonials, the British were exhausted by their efforts. In addition, they were low on ammunition.

Approaching the border separating the towns of Lincoln and Lexington, the British ran into an ambush by Captain Parker's Lexington militia. Lieutenant-Colonel Smith was knocked off his horse by a wound to his thigh, leaving Major John Pitcairn in command. Pitcairn sent light infantry companies to clear the hill of the militia positioned there. Although his forces succeeded in clearing two more hills, they were hit by a volley of musket fire by newly arrived militias. Pitcairn's horse was spooked by the shots, and Pitcairn's arm was injured when he was thrown to the ground.

The British were faring badly. Their commanders were injured, the ammunition was nearly gone, and the men were tired and thirsty. One officer noted, "We began to run rather than retreat in order. . . . We attempted to stop the men and form them two deep, but to no purpose, the confusion increased rather than lessened." Only when the officers stood in front of their men, with bayonets that they warned they would use if the men advanced, did the soldiers return to formation.

Because the British were so drained, and because ammunition stores were low, they could not continue to send out flanking parties, leaving the British vulnerable to militia fire. Luckily, Earl Percy arrived at 2:30 pm with a brigade of 1,000 men, rousing cheers from the exhausted and beleaguered British column.

Earl Percy recognized that the colonial fighting experience had been honed by their conflicts against the native tribes and the Canadians. Because they were fighting on familiar land that was dominated by hills and woods, the style worked for them. He described it as "very advantageous for their method of fighting." Even though the style was irregular, Percy acknowledged their perseverance. "Whoever looks upon them as an irregular mob will find himself much mistaken."

Chapter Six

Retreat from Concord

"By the rude bridge that arched the flood
Their flag to April's breeze unfurled
Here once the embattled farmers stood
And fired the shot heard round the world."

—Ralph Waldo Emerson

Earl Percy had not brought extra ammunition when he marched his troops out of Boston, nor had they brought ammunition for the artillery pieces they brought with them because Percy did not want the extra wagons to slow them down. Instead, General Gage sent two ammunition wagons after Percy, with an officer and thirteen soldiers as guards. However, the ammunition wagons had the ill-luck to run into a group of militiamen who were deemed too old to fight, as they were over 60 years old. The men mounted an ambush and ordered the soldiers to surrender the wagons. The British soldiers refused and kept riding. The militiamen, geriatric in age but not in zeal, began to fire, killing two sergeants and wounding the officer. The survivors ran and six surrendered to the militiamen.

Percy, oblivious to the drama surrounding the extra ammunition that General Gage had sent, focused his attention on the welfare of his men, which now numbered a force of 1,700 with the fresh troops as well as the weary veterans of the Concord fighting. Before resuming the march, the wounded were tended to and the others were able to eat, drink, and rest.

Around 3:30 pm, the soldiers mounted a formation that provided defensive positioning along the sides and rear of the column, and they headed to Lexington. Although militia forces continued to harass and fire at the British, Percy had arranged his forces tactically so that he could shift the units to where they were needed, forcing the militia to move outside of the British formation. Smith's weary men were in the middle of the column. Aware of the colonial style of fighting, Percy's rearguard was rotated every mile or so that his troops could have rest. There were flanking companies on both sides of the road with marines in front to clear the road.

The colonials now had Brigadier-General William Heath in command. The colonials perceived that they could not risk firing close upon the British column, or they could meet with cannon fire. Heath had conferred with Joseph Warren and other members of the Massachusetts Committee of Safety, and he felt that by moving in a ring and firing from a distance, they could still strike at the British without excessive risk. Militiamen on horseback would dismount, fire as the British approach, get back on their horses and gallop ahead to do the same thing again. Infantry added to the pressure on the sides of the columns, moving ahead when the column was out of range to re-engage the column down the road. Militiamen on foot fired from long range. As newly arriving militia units appeared, they were met by messengers from Heath directing them to designated locations along the road.

When Percy's men crossed from Lexington into the town of Menotomy (modern-day Arlington), more militia fired from a distance. Homeowners even fired from their own residences, while other homes served as sniper stations. House-to-house fighting turned especially savage as one house became the scene of conflict between a homeowner protecting his home and British troops. Eleven militia soldiers were killed in and around the house by British soldiers in what amounted to the bloodiest battle of the first day of the war. The house, called the Jason Russell House after its owner, still stands today and operates as a museum.

The British were falling into disorder, and Percy could not maintain control. The British soldiers were enraged by the killing that they had suffered from an enemy who seemed to strike while invisible. There were even suspicion that a British soldier had been scalped although his head wounds may have been caused by a hatchet. In retaliation, the British returned the savagery.

Percy ordered flanker companies to clear colonials out of the walls, trees, and buildings behind which they were hiding and firing, but the soldiers, upon entering a building, took vengeance on everyone they found, killing even unarmed people. General Gage's orders not to plunder or destroy property were forgotten. Taverns along the road were pillaged and the liquor stolen. The silver communion ware was stolen from a church and would only be recovered after it turned up in Boston for sale.

The tally of wounded and dead was actually worse in Menotomy and Cambridge than in Concord or Lexington on the day of the battle, with 40 British killed and 80 wounded, while the colonials saw 25 men killed and 9 wounded.

When the British crossed into Cambridge over the Menotomy River, Percy used his artillery pieces and flankers to strike against the fresh militiamen who had arrived. The Great Bridge had been dismantled under Heath's orders and could no longer be crossed, so Percy's troops approached the road to Charlestown by going down a narrow track, throwing off the waiting militia, now numbering 4,000 troops. When the colonial forces tried to move to a different hill for a better vantage point, Percy sent his cannon to the front and used up his remaining ammunition to disperse the militia.

More militiamen arrived but neglected to cut off the British access to Charlestown. Debate remains over whether the commander, Colonel Timothy Pickering, deliberately allowed the British to escape because he wanted to avoid war against Great Britain. Pickering later denied the charge, saying that his actions had been at Heath's behest, but Heath refuted this claim.

At any rate, by the time darkness was nearly falling, the British who were entering Charlestown were at a low ebb. Some had gone without sleep for two days, marching forty miles in twenty-one hours, eight of those hours spent as targets for colonial muskets. Fortunately, as they entered Charlestown, they were able to occupy stronger positions on the high ground, with heavy guns provided by the HMS *Somerset.* Gage sent two regiments to occupy the high ground and build fortifications that would end up never completed, although they would turn out to be useful two months later when the militia needed them before the Battle of Bunker Hill.

Chapter Seven

Aftermath

"The once-happy and peaceful plains of America are either to be drenched in blood or inhabited by slaves. Sad alternative! But can a virtuous man hesitate in his choice?"

—George Washington

When April 20 dawned in Boston, the city was encircled on three sides by a militia with over 15,000 men who had come from all over New England to protect the colonials against the British Army. The realization that the colony of Massachusetts had gone to war with the British Empire might not have reached the minds of all the inhabitants of the New World; still, the military forces on both sides realized that a dramatic turn of affairs had occurred. The size of the militia continued to increase as more men came from across New England, including forces from New Hampshire, Connecticut, and Rhode Island. A nation at war needed an army, and the Second Continental Congress realized that it had the nucleus of its military force in the New England militia.

For the British, the Battles of Lexington and Concord were dismal failures. They had not found enough weapons to make the effort worthwhile, and instead of establishing control over the area, they had inflamed it to the point where militiamen were pouring into the Boston region as word spread that they were needed. Still determined to maintain civility even in these trying circumstances, General Gage did not declare martial law in Boston, although as governor he was entitled to do so. He met with the city's elected leaders and persuaded them to surrender their personal weapons; in exchange, any inhabitants of the city who wanted to leave could do so.

Once again, the colonials proved their expertise in the art of public opinion, sending testimonies from British prisoners as well as militiamen to London on a ship faster than the one which was carrying Gage's official description of the conflict. Two weeks before Gage's report reached London, the colonial account was published in the city's newspapers. The politicians criticized Gage for the failure that had actually been instigated by short-sighted British government policies, and the British troops held their military leaders accountable for the failure.

To quell the rebellion, the government sent military reinforcements, along with three major-generals—John Burgoyne, Henry Clinton, and William Howe—whose professional ambitions would have delighted in the opportunity of replacing Gage in his position. The Crown recognized that not only did it have a rebellion to put down, but it also had the additional challenge of trying to bring an unruly population back into the fold. The political consciousness of the people of New England had been ignited by the events of April 19, and they would not be pacified.

Some of the men who would become known as the Founding Fathers recognized the change as well. John Adams, riding to the site of the battles, said, "the Die was cast, the Rubicon crossed." In Philadelphia, Thomas Paine was moved to support the cause although he had previously been dismissive of its purpose. He would later go on to write *Common Sense*, a stirring pamphlet in support of the American cause for independence. In his estate of Mount Vernon in Virginia, George Washington wrote to a friend that the choice was plain: "The once-happy and peaceful plains of America are either to be drenched in blood or inhabited by slaves. Sad alternative! But can a virtuous man hesitate in his choice?"

In 1836, Ralph Waldo Emerson wrote "Concord Hymn," memorializing the events at the North Bridge which turned a minor battle into the opening salvo of a long and bitter war between the colonists and the British government. Emerson had a grandfather who lived in Concord and had been an eyewitness to the battle. He wrote his poem as part of the dedication ceremony on July 4, 1837 for a monument that was placed at the North Bridge site.

Conclusion

By 1837, the Battles of Lexington and Concord had already entered into the national mythology of the young country. Although the battles themselves were of limited military significance, they were the setting for the war between a mighty empire and a rustic confederation of colonies who had yet to prove whether they could survive or thrive on the international stage. The ideas which were fomented in the American Revolution would be grafted onto an uprising in France not long after.

The Americans, in magnificent eloquence, informed King George III in the Declaration of Independence that he had failed to uphold the ideals of life, liberty, and happiness which were the right of every man. The Americans would have no king. The U.S. Constitution that was painstakingly carved out of pragmatism and idealism, a belief in the goodness of the human race, and a realization that men and women were all too prone to fail, became the law of the land in 1788. George Washington became the first president of the United States, and after two terms, he left the office and returned home to Mount Vernon, setting a precedent and avoiding any semblance of a dynastic presidency.

Back in 1775, however, the outcome of the conflict was still in grave doubt. The hostilities in Boston were far from over, and eventually, the fighting would spill into other the colonies. The fighting between the two foes would not end until the British surrendered at Yorktown in October 1781 and the peace treaty was signed in September 1783.

Could thirteen colonies become a nation? It seemed doubtful, but then, so was the likelihood of a provincial militia defeating trained British troops. Yet it happened at Concord.

Made in the USA
Middletown, DE
14 July 2023

35099658R00027